Flowers

Illustrated by René Mettler

A FIRST DISCOVERY BOOK

SCHOLASTIC INC.

Cartwheel
·B·O·O·K·S·®

New York   Toronto   London   Auckland   Sydney
Mexico City   New Delhi   Hong Kong   Buenos Aires

The crocus blooms when spring appears.

The orange pistil is hidden inside the flower.

pistil

stamen

The stamens
have pollen
in them.

Many flowers smell nice and have pretty colors. They attract insects. The insects like to eat the nectar or pollen.

Pollen gets on the insects' legs.
Then the insects carry the pollen
to the pistil of the next flower.

All flowers make seeds so that new plants can grow.

The dandelion starts as
a bud. Then it becomes a
flower. An insect leaves
some pollen on its pistils.

The petals dry up.

When the seeds
are ready,

they fly away
in the wind!

This is a strawberry plant.

Its green buds
open up into
little flowers.

The fruit grows
inside the center
of the flowers.

Soon, the petals fall off.
Now you can see ripe,
yummy strawberries!

All fruits come from a flower.
The fruits contain the seeds.

Apple

Eggplant

We call these vegetables, but they are also called fruits because they have seeds in them.

Green bean

Sometimes you can use parts of certain flowers to make foods, spices, and teas.

Saffron is the dried end of the crocus pistil. It is a spice often used in rice.

Saffron

Cloves

The clove is a dried flower bud. It is used in baking.

The artichoke is the bud of a plant with purple flowers.

Artichoke

Chamomile

Lime

Chamomile
and lime blossoms
are used to make tea.

Caper

Capers are also
flower buds —
they are used
in soups
and sauces.

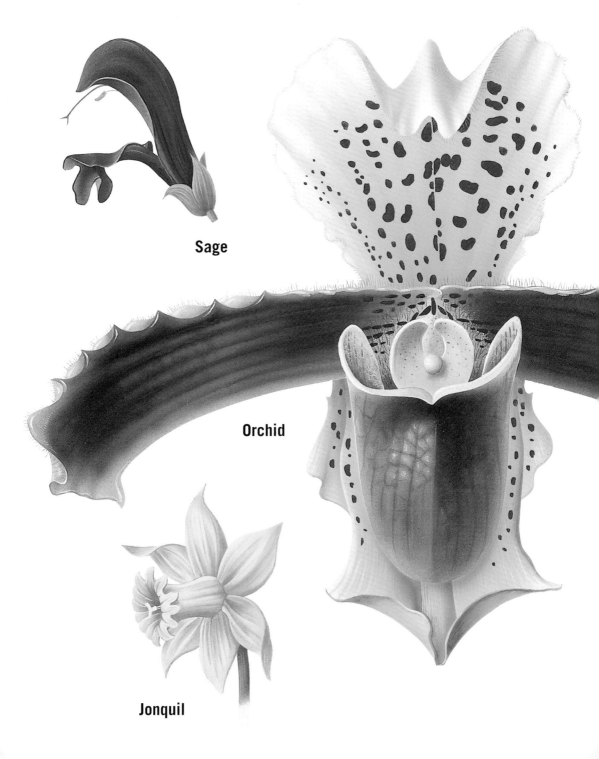

Sage

Orchid

Jonquil

Foxglove **Violet** **Clover**

Here are some well-known flowers. Look closely at the shape of their petals and their colors.

Bluebell **Iris**

Sunflowers are very big plants
that grow in very big fields.

Sunflower seeds
are ground up to
make cooking oil.

The sunflower gets its name
from the way the blossoms turn
to follow the movement of the sun.

The flowers in a flower shop are grown
by scientists called horticulturists.

In the countryside, you may see
the same flowers growing wild.

Daisy

Tiger lily

Hawthorn

Pansy

Dianthus

This is how to save your favorite flowers.

Press and dry them
between the pages
of a journal.
Then arrange the flowers
nicely and glue them
on a sheet of paper.

Buttercup

Edelweiss and bright blue gentians are
wild mountain flowers. They are very rare.
You must never, ever pick them.